About the book

Soaring high above Chesapeake Bay, a fish hawk spreads his powerful six-foot wings. Suddenly his wings fold and the dark brown bird plunges almost 100 feet into the water. A moment later he emerges clutching a large fish in his talons. Now he would return with his catch to the female and newborn chicks waiting in their nest. The fish hawk had begun the long day's work of feeding his family.

In BIOGRAPHY OF A FISH HAWK Burke Davis' informative text complements the precision of Jean Zallinger's illustrations. Together they portray the life cycle—from birth to often untimely death at the hands of man—of this amazing American bird.

A Nature Biography Book

Biography of a
FISH HAWK

by Burke Davis
illustrations by Jean Zallinger

G. P. Putnam's Sons / New York

To Chris Stinson

Text copyright © 1977 by Burke Davis
Illustrations Copyright © 1977 by Jean Zallinger
All rights reserved. Published simultaneously
in Canada by Longman Canada, Limited, Toronto.
PRINTED IN THE UNITED STATES OF AMERICA
Library of Congress Cataloging in Publication Data
Davis, Burke. Biography of a fish hawk.
Summary: Follows the life of a fish hawk from birth
to winter migration to adulthood and mating.
1. Ospreys—Juvenile literature. 2. Birds—
Chesapeake Bay—Juvenile literature. (1. Ospreys.
2. Hawks) I. Zallinger, Jean Day. II. Title.
QL969.F36D38   1977   598.9'1   76-49987
ISBN 0-399-61084-7 lib. bdg.

High in the air, into the spring dawn rose a
dark brown bird, soaring on powerful bent
wings. With his bright yellow eyes the bird
peered keenly into the waters far below him.

The white head and belly of the bird shone
in the early light. The great wings spread almost six feet, their tips and edges twisting and
turning, feeling for the currents of the breeze.

5

Suddenly the wings folded and the bird hurtled like a stone toward the water, a plunge of almost one hundred feet. The heavy body splashed into the water, disappeared for an instant with a wild flapping of wings, and rose slowly, clutching a large fish in his talons. He flapped toward the shore with a shrill whistle that carried far across Chesapeake Bay: "Whee-ew! Whee-ew!"

A fish hawk had begun a long day's work of feeding his family.

The hawk flapped down into the top of a pine tree and tore off the head of the fish and ate it. He then flew to a dead cedar tree on the beach. Here, atop a tall nest his mate was waiting with two downy white chicks and an unhatched egg. The male left the fish and flew back to the pine tree where he perched, keeping watch.

The female hawk ripped the fish into bits and fed her chicks. When they could eat no more, she ate the tail of the fish herself. As the sun rose she crouched with wings outstretched to shade the chicks. On the hottest days to come she would wet her breast in the water to help cool the chicks and the beautiful brown-splotched egg.

This egg would never hatch, no matter how long the female bird sat on it. It was the first egg she had laid in the spring, and it was filled with poison. The poison came from fish she had eaten in the bay, and it remained in the fat of her body. Most of this fat went into the first egg, so that the other two were not affected.

The poison actually came from far away. Deadly chemicals had been sprayed on farm crops to kill many insects. Some of the dead insects had fallen into small streams, and the fish had gobbled them up. These fish, in turn, had been eaten by larger fish, and the larger fish had moved down through the streams and rivers into the bay where the fish hawks hunted.

The fish hawk nest on the shore of the Chesapeake was a strange nest indeed. A tower of rubbish rose from the forks of the tree, up and up through the bare branches to the very top. From a distance it looked like a haystack hanging in the tree.

The great nest weighed more than five hundred pounds. It was four feet wide and eight feet tall, about as tall as the ceiling of a house. Generations of fish hawks—also known as

American ospreys—had used this nest for more than twenty years, building it higher each year. Like fish hawks all over the world, the strong-winged birds who lived in this nest had added almost everything they could carry—oars and poles, an old raincoat, a plank, a part of a fishing net, a rag doll, a fisherman's worn-out boot, a plastic baseball bat, a piece of garden

hose, cork floats from crab pots, a broom, a
bathing suit, a pair of trousers, a toy boat,
cornstalks, tin cans, bottles, and bunches of
seaweed. The nest was larger than the nests of
most fish hawks. But it was built in the man-
ner of all other nesting pairs of these birds. Fish
hawks return to the same nest year after year.

The hawks were not alone in their wonderful tower. The tall nest was really an apartment for wild creatures. The hawks had neighbors far below. On one side of the tower a pair of wrens nested in a small, neat hole. Not far away lived a family of red-winged blackbirds. A band of white-footed deer mice lived near the bottom of the nest. A father, mother, and more young mice than anyone could count scurried through small tunnels in the nest and peeped out from holes on every side.

The mice and smaller birds could not be seen from the high platform of the fish hawks, so they were not afraid. The big birds came and went without a glance at their small tenants.

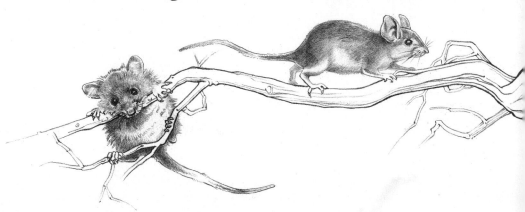

Beneath the cedar tree was a tangle of trees and shrubs, hollies and oaks, cypresses and bayberries, all stunted by the wind and twined with flowering vines. These thickets stretched away into a vast forest. Many days the fish hawks saw no signs of people, though they heard the sounds of a village a few miles away

—church bells and fire sirens and the horns of automobiles and boats. The boats of crabbers and fishermen sometimes came near, working in the waters of the bay. And at night the birds could see a tiny white light far out in the dark waters that winked slowly on top of a channel buoy to guide boats through the bay.

The hawk chicks grew rapidly. Eight or ten times each day the male hawk brought fish to the nest, and the two small birds ate hungrily.

Within three weeks the chicks began sprouting feathers on their heads, and then along their necks and wings. Now the older birds no longer tore their food into small bits, but dropped the whole fish into the nest so that the chicks could feed themselves. Not until the chicks were five weeks old did the female leave the nest to catch fish on her own.

When they were six weeks old, the chicks were fully feathered. Each feather was tipped with white as if it had been dipped in paint. Though the chicks were still helpless, they were often left alone in the nest. Their mother watched protectively from a nearby tree as the young birds grew more and more alert, bobbing their heads upright at the slightest sound and whistling weakly. Danger sometimes came near—an eagle soaring overhead, a flock of crows hunting for eggs, or a mysterious crackling in the undergrowth beneath the tree. A whistle from the mother hawk sent the chicks huddling down into the nest, hidden and still.

Late one afternoon when the father was fishing far away and the mother was keeping
watch, danger struck. A small black-masked
face peered from the thicket below. An old raccoon, the most deadly enemy of the fish hawks,
was on the prowl. The mother bird was dis-
tracted by a sound out on the bay, so she did
not see the hungry animal scramble onto the
huge pile of debris.

Deer mice fled in all directions. The wrens darted out and flew away. The female blackbird fluttered from her nest, leaving her eggs behind. The raccoon did not pause.

Climbing nimbly with long black paws that were like tiny human hands, the raider made his way upward. At last he raised himself to the edge of the hawk nest. First his nose appeared, then his masked face scarred from many battles. The two sleepy chicks were nodding with closed eyes. The mother hawk looked far across the bay, where night was beginning to fall.

The raccoon heaved his body into the nest. The chicks shrieked and beat their wings, but the animal seized one of them by the throat and tore the soft flesh with a snap of his jaw.

The mother hawk fell upon the raccoon in a fury, raking his back with her talons and gashing his head with her curved beak. She closed one of his small black eyes with a bloody slash. The raccoon wrenched himself from her grasp. The bird covered her young with outspread wings, raised one barbed claw, and hissed loudly. The wounded animal darted toward her with bared fangs and drew back swiftly, circling, seeking a chance to strike.

Without a sound the male hawk landed on the nest. The female darted forward and clutched the raccoon. Their bodies tumbled toward the ground with a beating of wings, snarling, and shrieking, until they crashed into the undergrowth. There was a sudden silence. The raccoon disappeared. The female hawk returned to the nest.

The wounded chick was dead and the egg had been crushed.

The remaining chick was soon almost as large as his mother. Every day he stood on the edge of the nest and beat his wings. Finally he was able to lift himself into the air, hovering a few inches above the nest before settling back into place, whistling in excitement. Each day he flapped longer and harder. He was fast growing stronger.

He flew at last when he was almost two months old, but it was not like the flight of his parents. He fluttered awkwardly as if about to fall to the earth, then rested for a time in a small tree, breathing rapidly with an open beak. He flapped back to the nest, squawking until he was perched safely on the platform. But a few moments later he was off again while his mother watched from her perch in the pine tree. A day later the chick flew into the pine beside her, and before the week was out he flew

over the bay, turning in broad circles, soaring
upward with the wind currents, and searching
the dark water beneath him as if he knew that
he must learn to live from the fish that swam
there.

The young bird's plumage was now streaked and spotted, his upper body cinnamon-brown with pale tips on his feathers. His head was creamy white, streaked with black, his breast light brown, and his legs and underparts white. He would be a year and a half old before he began to resemble his parents. But his feet were already huge, with heavy ridges and scales, so that he could hold the slippery bodies of fish. His curved talons were as sharp as they would ever be. The hooked black beak with its razor edges was very like that of his father. Already his eyes were much stronger than those of any human being. The young hawk could see far into the distance and even beneath the surface of the water over which he flew.

For two months or more the young hawk flew about, making longer and longer flights from the nest and returning each day to eat fish brought by the older birds. The fish did not appear so often now, for the parents seemed to know that their growing chick must learn to fish for himself. The young hawk sometimes stood on the nest whistling to show his hunger. But long hours would pass before one of them brought a fish.

One day as he flew over the bay the young hawk's sharp eyes caught the glint of fish moving below him. His wings beat rapidly as he hovered above the school of fish, and then, like his parents, he closed his wings and dove into the bay. His talons outstretched at the last instant, he raked the water for his prey. He struggled upward with empty claws. He was only six months old and was not quite able to catch his own food.

When autumn approached and his parents fed him less and less and he grew leaner and hungrier, the young hawk became a fisher. He circled tirelessly over the bay and inlets and rivers near the nest. As his eyes became keener he was able to see hundreds of fish when they drifted or darted just below the surface of the water. But though he splashed after them furiously day after day, the fish escaped. He was a fraction of a second too slow with his talons, or he was betrayed by his eyes, by the sweep of the tide, or by the gleam of sunlight on the water.

Each day during his fifth and sixth months he learned more about the place where he had been born. He came to know the tides; the movements of the fish, birds, and small animals in the marshes and woods; the storms and fogs.

He was often chased by small birds when he
flew near their nests, but went on his way until
they tired of the chase. He sometimes saw huge
eagles wheeling high above, powerful birds that
looked much like fish hawks from a great distance.

The young bird once struck a dead fish floating in the bay and bore it away to a treetop perch, but dropped it at once, for fish hawks do not eat carrion, only fresh fish or eels.

A day or so later he caught his first meal, a flounder trapped in shallow water near the shore which was easy prey for the hungry young bird. The hawk devoured the fish in the nest, hissing at his parents when they came near. It was his last catch for a long time.

On a blustery day in mid-September the young hawk made his first catch from the bay itself. He dove into a school of gray trout and caught a fine fat fish that weighed almost three pounds. His talons clutched the squirming body in an iron grip. The hawk struggled upward with his heavy burden. "Whee-ew!" he whistled. The young hawk did not trouble to look about him in the sky.

High overhead, hardly a speck in the blue, a bald eagle was soaring, waiting for just such a chance to steal a fish he could not catch for himself. The eagle plunged downward, screaming wildly. The huge bird zoomed so near that the young hawk dropped his trout and turned away in the rush of air from the eagle's wings. The eagle snatched the fish with ease, as he had so often from other fish hawks around the bay. The hungry young hawk joined his parents in their nest. He did not eat that night and woke often to call a few whistles of hunger. He began fishing once more with the first light of dawn.

In October when the nights grew longer and colder, the old hawks flew south in search of warmer weather. The young hawk stayed about the nest for a few more days, growing stronger with each flight. He caught fish more often now and did not lose them to eagles. When October was almost gone, he joined a flock of other young fish hawks who had flown down from the north. The half-grown chick was off on the first great flight of his life.

The hawks flew swiftly southward across the Carolinas and Georgia, stopping occasionally to rest and fish. Then they went on across Florida and made the long, tiring flight across the Gulf of Mexico.

Almost blinded by bolts of lightning and deafened by thunder, they flew through a storm at night. Some of the young birds beat against the gale winds until they tired and fell into the water where they drowned. Those who escaped were exhausted when they reached land once more. They rested and fished on the Mexican coast until they were strong again. Then they flew on southward over sandy deserts, mountains, jungles, and the sea. They passed over the Panama Canal and into South America.

The young hawks came at last to the wild upland country of Brazil, where they stopped for the winter. Life was easy once they learned to catch fish in the freshwater lakes and streams —and to avoid men with guns who came to hunt them. After a few of the flock had been killed by the roaring guns, the young birds retreated deeper into the wilderness where men did not follow.

The fish hawks moved northward again at
the approach of spring, the older males first,
followed by their mates. The younger birds remained behind to spend the next year fishing in
the wild rivers and lakes of the Brazilian jungles. The young hawk from the huge nest on
the Chesapeake often fished alone, but some
days he flew and roosted with other young
hawks. Though he would not become as deadly
a fisher as his father or mother until the end of
his second year, the young hawk caught fish
more easily with each passing month. He was
not often hungry now.

The young hawk seldom heard the hunters' guns in his second and third years, but there were other birds who did not live to return north. Some were shot by hunters, or died of diseases, or starved before they learned to fish well. It was the way of fish hawks, for of every ten young birds leaving their nests, no more than three or four would live to become adults and raise chicks of their own. Yet once fully grown, the great birds often live to the age of ten or twelve years.

The young hawk returned to the place of his birth on Chesapeake Bay for the fourth summer of his life, now fully grown and ready to mate for life. He was not alone for long. A few days after he had come back to his old fishing grounds, a flock of young female hawks passed over on their way north. One of these birds settled into a tall tree where the young male sat. She perched for a few moments, stretching her long wings, looking at the water and the forest and the young male.

He gave a low whistle and fluttered nearer to her. She preened her feathers and then sailed from the limb, wheeling over the water. The young male darted after her, but she turned swiftly upward, almost straight up into the sky, beating her wings rapidly and whistling loudly.

The young hawk chased her high over the bay, but as he drew near the female turned on him with outstretched claws and fell downward. The two birds tumbled toward the water, flapping and whistling until they almost struck the water, then soared upward again, only to fall and rise again. It was the courtship flight of the fish hawks.

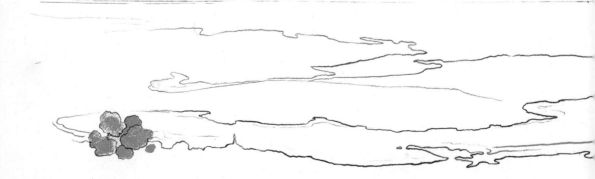

For more than half an hour the pair fluttered and wheeled and screamed above the bay before they flew off at last to perch side by side on their pine tree, snapping their beaks at each other now and then. A few moments later the male glided away. Drifting low above the water, he landed on the beach, where he seized a long, crooked dead branch in his claws and carried it back to the pine.

The female seized the branch and placed it across two limbs, tugging with her talons and beak until it rested snugly against the trunk. The male disappeared once more and returned with a barrel stave, which also went into place. He brought more branches and twigs, but there were many other things that only a nesting fish hawk would carry—a banana skin, a mop han-

dle, the body of a muskrat, a part of an old life preserver, a crushed fruit basket, and the skeleton of a pigeon with a few feathers flapping from a wing.

All of these things were carefully fitted into place by the two birds, who wedged each piece so that it would not move. A sturdy platform rose in the top of the pine tree.

Each day the work was halted when the birds suddenly sprang into the air and went soaring, wheeling, tumbling, and screaming through the sky in their courtship flights. Several times each day, as the female perched in a tree the male mounted her and deposited in her body the tiny sperms that fertilized the eggs she was to lay. Without these male sperms her eggs could not hatch and form chicks. But always after these brief moments, the fish hawks returned to the building of the nest. The male hawk carried his burdens from dawn to dusk with few pauses to rest or catch fish.

Within a week the nest was done. The female went into the marshes and brought back soft dead grasses to line a shallow bowl on top of the nest and began to sit there day and night. Soon there were three long pinkish, brown-splotched eggs in the nest:

And soon another brood of fish hawk chicks would come into the world, ready to begin new lives on the shore of the great bay.

The Author

Burke Davis lives near Williamsburg, Virginia, amid the marshes of Queens Creek, where fish hawks live through the long spring and summer seasons. He has written more than thirty books, including *Biography of a Leaf* and *Biography of a King Snake*. Mrs. Davis, a writer who also aids in her husband's research, is a veteran bird-watcher who has made a special study of the hawks of the eastern United States.

The Artist

Jean Zallinger was only thirteen when she started earning her own money to attend classes at the Museum School in Boston. Later she went to the Massachusetts School of Art and on to win a fellowship to the Yale School of Fine Arts. There she met her husband, Rudolph, the well-known naturalist painter who won a Pulitzer Prize for painting for his mural of dinosaurs in the Peabody Museum of Natural History at Yale. She now teaches at the Paier Art School in Connecticut. Mrs. Zallinger illustrated *Biography of a Leaf* and *Biography of an Armadillo*.

j598.2 Davis, Burke
DAV
    Biography of a fish
    hawk

780789

DATE		

© THE BAKER & TAYLOR CO.